Introduction 1

Chapter 1: Understanding the Importance of Email Lists 3

Chapter 2: Creating an Irresistible Lead Magnet. 6

Chapter 3: Optimizing Your Website for Email Signups 11

Chapter 4: Leveraging Content Marketing for List Growth 14

Chapter 5: Using Social Media to Grow Your Email List 18

Chapter 6: Implementing Referral and Sharing Strategies 22

Chapter 7: Hosting Webinars and Events to Drive List Growth 26

Chapter 8: Collaborating with Influencers and Partners 32

Chapter 9: Running Contests and Giveaways. 36

Chapter 10: Analyzing and Optimizing Your Email List Growth Strategy 41

Introduction

Welcome to "The Ultimate Guide on How to Grow Your Email List!" I'm thrilled to have you here, and I'm confident that by the end of this book, you'll be equipped with all the strategies and techniques you need to build and grow a robust email list. An email list is a goldmine for any business. It's a direct line to your audience, allowing you to engage with them effectively, nurture relationships, and ultimately drive conversions. In this digital age, where social media platforms and other marketing channels are constantly changing, email remains a reliable and effective tool for communication.

Unlike social media, where algorithms decide who sees your content, email gives you direct access to your audience's inbox. This means your message reaches them without any interference, ensuring better engagement and response rates.

In this book, we'll explore various aspects of email list growth. We'll start by understanding why building an email list is crucial for your business's success. Then, we'll dive into strategies like creating irresistible lead magnets, optimizing your website for email signups, leveraging content marketing, and using social media. We'll also cover implementing referral and sharing strategies, hosting webinars and events, collaborating with influencers and partners, running contests and giveaways, and analyzing and optimizing your email list growth strategy.

Each chapter is packed with practical tips, insights, and actionable steps that you can take to enhance your email list growth efforts. Our goal is to help you not only build a substantial email list but also cultivate an engaged and loyal audience who eagerly awaits your messages.

Whether you're a seasoned entrepreneur looking to fine-tune your email marketing strategy or a new business owner just starting out, this book will be your ultimate guide to growing your email list and driving business success.

So, without further ado, let's dive into the world of email list growth and discover the strategies that will take your business to new heights.

Chapter 1: Understanding the Importance of Email Lists

Let's dive into a topic that's absolutely essential for any entrepreneur looking to grow their business: email lists. In this chapter, we'll explore why building and nurturing an email list is so important, and how it can be a game-changer for your business.

Why Email Lists Matter

Picture this: You have a direct line to your audience, right into their personal inboxes. That's what email marketing offers. Unlike social media or other marketing channels where algorithms control visibility, email allows you to reach your subscribers directly. This direct connection helps to establish a stronger bond and builds trust between you and your audience.

Think about it: when you post something on social media, there's no guarantee that all your followers will see it. Social media platforms frequently change their algorithms, which can drastically affect your reach. But with an email list, you own your list. You decide when and what to send. This control is invaluable for your marketing efforts.

Increased Engagement and

Conversion

One of the biggest perks of having an email list is the boost in engagement and conversion rates. When someone signs up for your email list, they're signaling that they're genuinely interested in what you have to offer. This means they're more likely to open your emails, read your content, and take action.

With an engaged email list, you're in a prime position to drive conversions. Whether you're launching a new product, sharing valuable content, or offering exclusive discounts, email lets you directly communicate with your audience and prompt them to act. This direct line of communication is far more effective than hoping your social media posts get noticed.

Building Long-Term Relationships

Email lists aren't just about one-off promotions or quick sales. They're a powerful tool for building long-term relationships with your audience. By consistently providing value through your emails, you can establish yourself as an authority in your industry. Your subscribers will start to see you as a trusted source of information.

When your audience trusts you and values your expertise, they're more likely to stay loyal to your brand and make repeat purchases.

These long-term relationships can lead to higher customer lifetime value, which is a fancy way of saying your customers will keep coming back, helping your business grow over time.

Targeted Communication

Another major advantage of email lists is the ability to segment and target your communication. Not all subscribers are the same, and sending personalized, relevant content to specific segments of your list can significantly improve your results.

By understanding your audience's preferences and interests, you can tailor your emails to meet their specific needs. This targeted approach increases the likelihood of engagement and conversions, as your subscribers feel that your content is speaking directly to them.

Conclusion

In this chapter, we've covered why email lists are so important for entrepreneurs. Email lists give you direct access to your audience's inboxes, allowing you to build long-term relationships and drive engagement and conversions. By appreciating the significance of email marketing, you can leverage its power to grow your business and achieve your goals. In the upcoming chapters, we'll dive deeper into specific strategies and tactics for growing your email list.

Chapter 2: Creating an Irresistible Lead Magnet

In this chapter, we're diving into the fascinating world of lead magnets and exploring how you can use them to grow your email list effectively. A lead magnet is essentially a valuable piece of content or a resource that you offer to your audience in exchange for their email address. Think of it as a little incentive or bribe to encourage visitors to subscribe to your email list.

Understanding the Value of Lead Magnets

Lead magnets are a crucial element of any successful email list growth strategy. They provide a compelling reason for your target audience to willingly opt-in and share their contact information. By offering a valuable and relevant lead magnet, you can attract the right people to join your email list, ensuring that you build a quality and engaged subscriber base.

The magic of lead magnets lies in their ability to provide immediate gratification. People are often hesitant to part with their email addresses, but when they see the potential value in what you're offering, they're much more likely to take that step. Moreover, lead magnets position you as an expert or authority in your niche, helping to establish trust with your audience.

Types of Lead Magnets

There are several types of lead magnets you can create to entice your audience and convince them to join your email list. Here are some popular and effective examples:

Ebooks and Guides:
These are comprehensive resources that address a specific problem or educate your audience on a particular topic. Make sure the content is well-researched, practical, and packed with value.

Checklists and Cheat Sheets:
Offer a simple, easy-to-follow checklist or cheat sheet that helps your audience streamline a process or achieve a particular goal. Their concise format is appealing and provides immediate value.

Templates and Worksheets:
Provide pre-designed templates or interactive worksheets that assist your audience in completing a task or organizing information. These tools save time and offer convenience.

Video Tutorials:
Create video content that teaches your audience a skill or demonstrates how to

achieve a desired outcome. Videos are engaging and allow for a more personal connection with your audience.

Case Studies and Success Stories:
Share real-life examples or success stories that showcase how your products or services have helped others achieve their goals. This type of lead magnet inspires and builds credibility.

Creating an Effective Lead Magnet

To ensure your lead magnet is truly irresistible, it's important to consider a few key factors:

Relevance:
Your lead magnet should align with your target audience's needs and pain points. Conduct thorough research to understand their desires and preferences so you can create a lead magnet that is highly appealing.

Value:
Deliver high-quality and valuable content that exceeds your audience's expectations. The more valuable the lead magnet, the more motivated your audience will be to join your email list.

Visual Appeal:
Use visually appealing design elements such as engaging graphics, clean layouts, and

professional images. Aesthetically pleasing lead magnets are more likely to attract attention and be shared.

Clear Call-to-Action:
Clearly explain the benefits of your lead magnet and explicitly state what your audience needs to do to access it. Guide them through the opt-in process with a prominent and persuasive call-to-action.

Promoting Your Lead Magnet

Creating a compelling lead magnet is just one part of the equation; promoting it effectively is equally important. Here are some strategies to attract attention and generate sign-ups:

Website Optimization:
Place prominent opt-in forms and call-to-action buttons on your website, making it easy for visitors to subscribe. Consider using pop-ups or slide-ins to capture attention.

Landing Pages:
Create dedicated landing pages specifically designed to promote your lead magnet. Optimize these pages with persuasive copy, attractive visuals, and a clear opt-in form for maximum conversions.

Social Media Promotion:
Leverage your social media platforms to

promote your lead magnet. Create engaging posts with captivating visuals and direct your audience to a landing page or opt-in form.

Collaborations:
Partner with influencers or complementary businesses to promote your lead magnet to their audience. This allows you to tap into a wider network and reach potential subscribers who may be interested in your content.

Guest Blogging:
Write guest blog posts for relevant websites or industry publications and include a link to your lead magnet in your author bio or within the content itself. This exposes your lead magnet to a new audience and drives traffic to your website.

Email Signature:
Add a call-to-action and a link to your lead magnet in your email signature. This way, every email you send becomes an opportunity to promote and drive sign-ups.

Creating an irresistible lead magnet is a crucial step in growing your email list. By providing value upfront and offering something of interest to your audience, you can entice them to share their contact information. In the next chapter, we will discuss optimizing your website for email signups.

Chapter 3: Optimizing Your Website for Email Signups

Your website is an incredibly powerful tool for growing your email list. By strategically optimizing your site for email signups, you can significantly enhance your ability to capture leads and convert casual visitors into loyal subscribers. In this chapter, we will delve into a range of strategies and best practices that will help you fine-tune your website to maximize email signups.

Create a Prominent Signup Form

The very first step in optimizing your website for email signups is ensuring that your signup form is prominently displayed. It should be placed in a highly visible location, such as at the top of your homepage or within the sidebar. Using contrasting colors and eye-catching design elements can help make the form stand out even more.

Consider incorporating pop-up or slide-in forms to grab the attention of your visitors. These types of forms can be triggered based on user behavior, such as when a user is about to leave your site (exit-intent) or after they've spent a certain amount of time browsing. However, be careful not to overdo it with intrusive tactics that might annoy your visitors and disrupt their experience on your site.

Craft Compelling Copy

When it comes to optimizing your website for email signups, the copy you use is crucial. You need to create compelling content that clearly communicates the value of subscribing to your email list. Capture your visitors' attention by highlighting the benefits they will receive by joining your list. This could include exclusive content, special discounts, or access to valuable resources.

Use persuasive language and strong call-to-action buttons to motivate visitors to take the plunge and sign up. Be clear and concise about why they should subscribe and what they can expect to receive. Avoid using generic or vague messaging that might not resonate with your target audience.

Offer Attractive Incentives

Incentives can be a game-changer when it comes to boosting your email signup rates. Consider offering a lead magnet or some form of exclusive content as a reward for subscribing. This might be a free ebook, a downloadable template, or a discount code for your products or services.

Make sure to clearly communicate this incentive throughout your website and on your signup form. Let visitors know exactly what they will receive by subscribing and emphasize how this incentive will help solve a specific problem or meet a particular need they have.

Optimize for Mobile Users

With the increasing prevalence of mobile device usage, it's essential to ensure your website is optimized for mobile users. This means your signup form and overall website design need to be mobile-friendly and responsive. Test your website on a variety of devices and screen sizes to ensure a smooth and seamless user experience.

Simplify the signup process for mobile users by minimizing the number of form fields and making it as easy as possible for them to subscribe while on the go. Consider using autofill features to speed up the process of entering information.

Utilize Social Proof

Social proof is an incredibly effective tool for boosting your email signup rates. Showcasing testimonials, reviews, or your social media follower counts can help demonstrate the credibility and popularity of your brand. This can build trust with your visitors and encourage them to subscribe to your email list.

Highlight any impressive numbers or statistics related to your email list, such as the number of subscribers you have or your average open rate. This can create a sense of urgency and

FOMO (fear of missing out), motivating visitors to sign up.

By implementing these strategies and best practices, you can effectively optimize your website for email signups and significantly increase your chances of converting visitors into engaged subscribers. Remember to regularly test and analyze your signup rates to identify areas for improvement and continually refine your approach.

Chapter 4: Leveraging Content Marketing for List Growth

Growing your email list is a fundamental aspect of successful marketing, and content marketing plays a pivotal role in achieving this goal. By creating and sharing valuable content, you can attract a broader audience and convert them into loyal subscribers. In this chapter, we'll delve into various techniques and strategies for leveraging content marketing to expand your email list.

The Power of High-Quality Content

First and foremost, high-quality content is essential for attracting and retaining subscribers. Your content should provide real value to your audience by addressing their pain points, answering their questions, and offering practical solutions. When you consistently deliver valuable content, you position yourself as an authority in your industry, fostering trust and loyalty among your audience.

Identifying Your Target Audience

Before diving into content creation, it's crucial to identify your target audience. Understanding who they are—their demographics, interests, and preferences—will help you create content that truly resonates with them. Conduct market research, analyze your existing audience, and utilize tools like Google Analytics to gain deeper insights into who your target audience is and what they want.

Creating a Content Strategy

A well-defined content strategy is your roadmap to creating and distributing content that aligns with your goals and resonates with your audience. Start by setting clear objectives for your content marketing efforts. Are you aiming to increase brand awareness, drive traffic to your website, or generate leads? Once you have established your goals, create an editorial calendar to plan and organize your content production and distribution. This will ensure that you stay consistent and on track.

Creating Valuable and Engaging Content

Quality over quantity is the golden rule of content marketing. Your content should be valuable, engaging, and shareable. Explore different content formats such as blog posts, videos, infographics, podcasts, and eBooks to cater to various preferences. Use storytelling techniques to make your content more engaging, incorporate visuals to enhance understanding, and ensure your content is easy to consume. Additionally, remember to optimize your content for search engines to increase its visibility and reach a wider audience.

Promoting Your Content

Creating great content is only half the battle; promoting it effectively is equally important. Utilize different marketing channels to distribute your content and attract new subscribers. Share your content on social media platforms, participate in relevant online communities, collaborate with influencers, and consider guest blogging on industry-leading websites. Encourage your audience to share your content by incorporating social sharing buttons and calls-to-action (CTAs) within your content.

Gating Valuable Content

Gating valuable content can be a highly effective strategy for growing your email list. Offer exclusive access to premium content, such as in-depth guides, templates, or webinars, in exchange for email addresses. This approach not only provides additional value to your audience but also captures their contact information, enabling you to nurture these leads further.

Measuring and Optimizing

To gauge the effectiveness of your content marketing efforts, it's essential to track key metrics such as website traffic, engagement rates, and conversion rates. Utilize analytics tools and email marketing software to gain insights into your content's performance. Make data-driven decisions to refine your strategy. Experiment with different content formats, headlines, and distribution channels to optimize your approach and maximize list growth.

By effectively leveraging content marketing, you can attract a larger and more engaged audience to your email list. Remember to consistently create valuable content, identify your target audience, develop a solid content strategy, promote your content widely, gate valuable resources, and measure and optimize your efforts. With a well-executed content marketing strategy, you can experience significant growth in your email list, ultimately driving business success.

Chapter 5: Using Social Media to Grow Your Email List

In today's digital age, social media platforms have evolved into powerful tools that businesses can utilize to reach and engage with their target audience. If used effectively, social media can significantly contribute to the growth of your email list. In this chapter, we'll delve into various strategies and tips on how to harness the power of social media to expand your email list.

The Power of Social Media

Platforms like Facebook, Instagram, Twitter, LinkedIn, and Pinterest offer incredible opportunities to connect with your audience and encourage them to subscribe to your email list. With millions, and in some cases, billions of active users, these platforms provide the perfect setting to reach a vast and varied audience.

1. Promote Your Lead Magnets

One highly effective method for growing your email list through social media is by promoting your lead magnets. Remember those valuable resources we discussed back in Chapter 2?

Now is the time to showcase them on your social media channels. Create compelling posts that highlight the benefits of your lead magnets and include a clear call-to-action inviting users to subscribe to your email list to access them. To grab attention and increase engagement, use eye-catching visuals like images or videos.

2. Run Social Media Contests and Giveaways

Running contests and giveaways on social media is another powerful tactic to grow your email list. Design a contest or giveaway that requires participants to provide their email addresses to enter. This approach not only helps you grow your email list but also generates excitement and buzz around your brand, encouraging social sharing. Just be sure to comply with the platform's guidelines and regulations when organizing contests.

3. Collaborate with Influencers and Partners

Collaborating with influencers and strategic partners in your industry can be an exceptionally effective way to expand your reach and grow your email list via social media. Identify influencers or brands that have a similar target audience and propose a win-win collaboration opportunity. For example, you could co-create valuable content together or host a joint webinar. By leveraging their established following, you can boost brand awareness and drive more subscribers to your email list.

4. Optimize Your Social Media Profile and Bio

Ensure that your social media profiles are optimized to encourage users to subscribe to your email list. Include a clear and compelling call-to-action in your profile's bio section, along with a link to your signup or landing page. Additionally, consider using a pinned post or a featured section to promote your lead magnet or offer exclusive content to those who subscribe.

5. Engage and Interact with Your Audience

Building a strong and engaged community on social media is crucial for growing your email list. Actively engage with your audience by responding to comments, direct messages, and inquiries. Encourage discussions, ask questions, and foster meaningful conversations around your brand and industry. Engaging with your audience not only helps build relationships but also creates opportunities to convert social media followers into email subscribers.

6. Leverage Social Media Advertising

If you have the budget, social media

advertising can be an incredibly effective strategy for growing your email list. Platforms like Facebook and Instagram offer robust targeting options, allowing you to reach a specific audience based on demographics, interests, behaviors, and more. Create targeted ads that promote your lead magnets or direct users to a dedicated landing page optimized for email signups.

Conclusion

Social media platforms provide numerous opportunities to grow your email list and expand your reach. By promoting your lead magnets, running contests and giveaways, collaborating with influencers, optimizing your social media profiles, engaging with your audience, and leveraging social media advertising, you can effectively drive more signups to your email list. Remember to consistently analyze and optimize your social media strategies to ensure maximum results.

In the next chapter, we'll explore more advanced techniques and insights to help you take your email marketing to the next level. Stay tuned!

Chapter 6: Implementing Referral and Sharing Strategies

Welcome to Chapter 6, where we're going to dive into the exciting world of referral and sharing strategies. These strategies can be incredibly powerful tools for growing your email list, expanding your reach, and attracting new subscribers. By leveraging the trust and influence of your loyal followers, you can effectively drive list growth.

The Power of Referrals

Let's start by talking about referrals. Referrals are recommendations made by your satisfied customers or subscribers to their friends, family, or colleagues. People inherently trust the opinions and recommendations of those they know, making referrals an instrumental tool in growing your email list.

So, how can you effectively implement a referral strategy? One of the most effective methods is by offering incentives or rewards for referrals. For instance, you can provide your existing subscribers with a unique referral link or code that they can share with others. When someone signs up using that referral link or code, both the referrer and the new subscriber can receive a reward. This reward could be a discount on a product, access to exclusive content, or any other enticing offer.

To make it easier for your subscribers to share their referral links, include social sharing buttons in your emails and on your website. These buttons allow subscribers to effortlessly share your content with their social networks. You can also create pre-written social media posts that your subscribers can copy and paste onto their profiles, making the sharing process even more straightforward.

Utilizing Social Sharing

In addition to referrals, social sharing can significantly amplify your list growth efforts. When your subscribers share your content on their social media platforms, it exposes your brand and email list to their entire network of connections, potentially leading to new subscribers.

To encourage social sharing, focus on creating valuable and share-worthy content that resonates with your audience. This could include informative blog posts, engaging videos, or eye-catching infographics. Make it easy for your subscribers to share your content by including social sharing buttons on your website and within your emails.

You can also create incentives for social

sharing. For example, you might offer a giveaway or contest entry to anyone who shares your content on their social media profiles and tags your brand. This strategy not only encourages sharing but also increases your brand's visibility to a wider audience.

Tracking and Analyzing Referrals and Sharing

Now, let's talk about tracking and analyzing your referral and sharing strategies. It's crucial to measure the success of these efforts to understand what's working and what needs improvement.

Start by monitoring the number of referrals you receive and identifying the sources of those referrals. This will help you determine which channels are driving the most signups and where you should focus your efforts.

For tracking social shares, use social media analytics tools to see which posts are generating the most engagement and shares. This data will provide insights into the type of content that resonates with your audience, guiding your future content creation efforts.

Analyzing the data will also help you identify your most influential referrers or sharers. These individuals can be invaluable to your strategy. Reach out to them, express your gratitude for their support, and consider building stronger relationships with them. Influential individuals in your industry can lead to further opportunities for collaborations and partnerships.

Conclusion

Implementing referral and sharing strategies can help your email list grow exponentially. By tapping into the trust and influence of your existing subscribers, you can expand your reach and attract new subscribers. Encourage referrals by offering incentives and make it easy for your subscribers to share your content through social sharing buttons. Track and analyze the data to uncover insights and optimize your strategies. With the power of referrals and social sharing, you can take your email list growth efforts to new heights.

Chapter 7: Hosting Webinars and Events to Drive List Growth

Webinars and events are incredible tools for entrepreneurs looking to connect with their audience, provide valuable content, and ultimately grow their email list. These interactive experiences allow you to showcase your expertise, engage with your audience in real-time, and collect email addresses from interested participants. Let's explore the strategies and best practices for hosting webinars and events that drive list growth.

The Benefits of Hosting Webinars and Events

Webinars and events offer numerous advantages for entrepreneurs eager to expand their email list. Here are some key benefits:

1. Building Credibility and Authority: Hosting webinars and events positions you as an expert in your industry. By delivering valuable content and insights, you establish credibility and authority, encouraging attendees to subscribe to your email list for more valuable resources.
2. Engaging with Your Target Audience: Webinars and events create a platform

for direct interaction with your audience. You can answer their questions, address their pain points, and provide personalized advice. This engagement helps build rapport with your audience and increases the likelihood of them joining your email list.
3. Showcasing Your Products or Services: Webinars and events provide an opportunity to demonstrate the value of your products or services. Offering exclusive discounts or bonuses to attendees can incentivize them to join your email list, enabling you to nurture leads and convert them into loyal customers.
4. Collecting Valuable Data:
During webinars and events, you can collect valuable data, such as email addresses and demographic information, from participants. This data allows you to segment your email list and tailor personalized content that resonates with specific audience segments.

Planning and Promoting Your Webinar or Event

To ensure a successful webinar or event that drives list growth, it's essential to plan and promote it effectively. Here are some steps to consider:

1. Define Your Goals and Objectives:
   Before hosting a webinar or event, clearly define your goals and objectives. Are you aiming to increase your email list by a certain percentage? Or perhaps you want to generate leads for a new product launch? By setting specific goals, you can plan your content and promotional strategies accordingly.
2. Choose a Relevant Topic:
   Select a topic that aligns with your audience's interests and addresses their pain points. Research popular industry trends, conduct surveys, or analyze feedback from your current subscribers to identify relevant topics that will attract a larger audience.
3. Create Compelling Content:
   Develop engaging and valuable content for your webinar or event. Structure your presentation in a way that keeps participants interested and provides actionable takeaways. Incorporate visuals, case studies, and real-life examples to enhance the learning experience.
4. Select the Right Platform:
   Choose a reliable webinar or event platform that suits your needs. There are several options available, such as

Zoom, GoToWebinar, and WebEx. Consider factors like the number of attendees, interactive features, and ease of registration and email collection.
5. Promote Your Webinar or Event: Create a comprehensive promotion strategy to generate buzz and maximize attendance. Leverage your email list, social media channels, blog/newsletter updates, and collaborations with influencers or partners. Create visually appealing graphics and compelling copy to capture attention and entice potential attendees.

Driving List Growth During Your Webinar or Event

During your webinar or event, take advantage of the captive audience to drive list growth. Here are some tactics to implement:

1. Offer Exclusive Content or Resources: Provide valuable content or resources that are exclusive to attendees. This could include downloadable guides, templates, or industry reports. By offering these incentives, you can encourage participants to subscribe to your email list to gain access to additional valuable content.
2. Implement Interactive Features: Engage participants through interactive

features such as live polls, Q&A sessions, or chat functionality. This not only enhances the attendee experience but also allows you to collect email addresses and follow up with participants after the event.
3. Include Call-to-Actions (CTAs): Incorporate compelling CTAs throughout your webinar or event. Encourage attendees to sign up for your email list to receive updates, notifications of future events, or exclusive offers. Clearly communicate the benefits of joining your list and make it easy for participants to subscribe.

Follow-up and Nurturing

After the webinar or event, it's crucial to follow up with your attendees and nurture the relationship with your new subscribers. Here are some steps to consider:

1. Send Thank You Emails:
   Send personalized thank you emails to participants within 24-48 hours after the event. Express your gratitude for their attendance and include a brief summary of the key takeaways. This email provides an opportunity to include a CTA for joining your email list if they haven't already.
2. Provide Additional Resources:

Share additional resources related to the webinar or event topic. This could be a recording of the webinar, relevant blog posts, or links to further reading. By providing valuable content, you continue to establish yourself as an authority and keep your audience engaged.
3. Segment Your List and Tailor Content: Segment your new subscribers based on their webinar or event attendance and specific interests. This allows you to send targeted and relevant content that resonates with each segment. Personalization increases engagement and helps to nurture leads into conversions.
4. Evaluate and Optimize:
Analyze the success of your webinar or event by tracking the number of email signups, attendee feedback, and conversion rates. Use this data to improve future webinars or events and refine your email list growth strategy.

Conclusion

Hosting webinars and events is an effective strategy for entrepreneurs to grow their email lists and engage with their target audience. By carefully planning and promoting your webinar or event, providing valuable content, and following up with attendees, you can drive list growth and increase conversions. Remember to continuously optimize your strategy based on data and feedback to ensure long-term success.

Chapter 8: Collaborating with Influencers and Partners

Collaborating with influencers and partners is a powerful strategy for growing your email list. By partnering with individuals or businesses with a large and engaged audience, you can tap into their network and reach a wider audience. This chapter will explore the benefits of influencer and partner collaborations and provide actionable tips on how to implement this strategy effectively.

The Benefits of Collaborating with Influencers and Partners

Collaborating with influencers and partners can offer several benefits for growing your email list:

Increased Reach and Exposure

Influencers and partners already have a dedicated following that trusts their recommendations. By collaborating with them, you can leverage their reach to promote your email list and gain exposure to a new audience. This can significantly boost your list growth and brand visibility.

Social Proof and Credibility

When influencers or respected partners endorse your brand and recommend joining your email list, it lends credibility and social proof to your offerings. This can help build trust with their audience and encourage more sign-ups for your email list.

Targeted Audience

When selecting collaborators, it is important to choose influencers or partners whose audience aligns with your target demographic. By collaborating with individuals or businesses that share a similar target audience, you can ensure that your message reaches the right people who are more likely to be interested in what you have to offer.

Strategies for Collaborating with Influencers and Partners

Now that you understand the benefits, let's explore some actionable strategies for collaborating with influencers and partners to grow your email list:

Identify Relevant Influencers and Partners

Start by identifying influencers or partners who have a significant following and whose audience aligns with your target market. Look for individuals or businesses that share similar values and have a genuine interest in your niche. You can use social media platforms, industry-specific directories, and online searches to find suitable collaborators.

Reach Out and Build Relationships

Once you've identified potential collaborators, reach out to them and propose a partnership. Personalize your outreach and explain how collaborating with you can benefit their audience. Offer something of value, such as exclusive content or discounts, to incentivize their participation. Building genuine relationships with influencers and partners is key to successful collaborations.

Co-create Valuable Content

Collaborate with influencers and partners to create valuable content that resonates with their audience and aligns with your email list goals. This can include guest blog posts, co-hosted webinars, or joint social media campaigns. By providing valuable content, you can attract their audience's attention and drive sign-ups to your email list.

Offer Exclusive Incentives

To encourage their audience to join your email list, consider offering exclusive incentives such as access to premium content, early access to product launches, or exclusive discounts.

These incentives create a sense of urgency and exclusivity, motivating their audience to subscribe to your list.

Promote Collaborations on Multiple Channels

To maximize the impact of your collaborations, promote them on multiple channels. Share the collaboration on your website, blog, social media platforms, and through email marketing. This multi-channel approach will help increase visibility and attract more potential subscribers.

Track and Measure Results

As with any marketing strategy, it is important to track and measure the results of your collaborations. Monitor the growth of your email list during and after the collaboration, and analyze the engagement and conversion rates of the new subscribers. This data will help you evaluate the success of your collaborations and make informed decisions for future partnerships.

In Conclusion

Collaborating with influencers and partners can be a highly effective strategy for growing your email list. By leveraging their reach, credibility, and targeted audience, you can significantly boost your list growth and brand visibility. Remember to identify relevant collaborators, build strong relationships, co-create valuable content, offer exclusive incentives, promote collaborations on multiple channels, and track and measure your results. Implementing these strategies will help you harness the power of influencers and partners to grow your email list and drive business success.

Chapter 9: Running Contests and Giveaways

Running contests and giveaways can be an incredibly effective strategy for growing your email list. By offering something of value to your audience, you can incentivize them to provide their email addresses and engage with your brand. In this chapter, we'll delve into the benefits of running contests and giveaways and provide practical tips on how to execute them successfully.

Benefits of Running Contests and Giveaways

Contests and giveaways come with a host of benefits when it comes to growing your email list:

Increase Brand Awareness

1. Contests and giveaways are fantastic for increasing brand visibility and awareness. When you run a contest or giveaway, people are more likely to share your content with their friends and followers. This not only expands your reach but also attracts new potential subscribers.

Generate Excitement and Engagement

2. There's something about the chance to win a prize that creates a sense of excitement and anticipation. By offering a chance to win something valuable, you can capture your audience's attention and encourage them to engage actively with your brand. This engagement often leads to an increase in email signups.

Build Trust and Loyalty

3. Offering valuable prizes demonstrates your commitment to providing value to your audience. This can help build trust and loyalty among your existing subscribers, encouraging them to stay subscribed and refer others to join your email list.

Collect Valuable Data

4. Contests and giveaways provide an excellent opportunity to collect valuable data about your audience. By asking for specific information during the entry process, such as email addresses, names, and demographic information, you can gather insights that inform your marketing strategy and help you tailor your messages to your target audience

more effectively.

Tips for Running Successful Contests and Giveaways

To ensure the success of your contests and giveaways, consider the following tips:

Set Clear Goals and Objectives

1. Before launching a contest or giveaway, it's crucial to define your goals and objectives. Are you aiming to increase your email list by a certain percentage? Are you looking to generate buzz around a new product or service? Setting clear goals will help you determine the best approach and measure the success of your campaign.

Choose Relevant Prizes

2. Select prizes that are highly relevant to your target audience. Ideally, the prizes should align with your brand and the interests of your subscribers. By offering prizes that are valuable and desirable, you increase the likelihood of attracting participants who are genuinely interested in your offerings and more likely to become long-term subscribers.

Determine Entry Requirements

3. Decide on the entry requirements for your contest or giveaway. For example, you may require participants to provide their email address, follow you on social media, share your content, or answer a question. While you want to make it easy for people to enter, ensure that the entry requirements align with your goals and objectives.

Promote Your Contest or Giveaway

4. Promotion is key to the success of your contest or giveaway. Utilize your website, blog, social media platforms, email newsletters, and any other relevant channels to spread the word. Create compelling graphics and copy to capture attention and entice people to enter. Consider using paid advertising on social media or partnering with influencers to reach a wider audience.

Follow Legal Guidelines

5. When running contests and giveaways, it's important to familiarize yourself with the legal requirements and regulations in your jurisdiction. Ensure that your

contest or giveaway complies with any necessary rules regarding eligibility, disclosure, and prize distribution. Consulting with a legal professional can help you navigate any potential legal concerns.

Track and Analyze Results

6. After your contest or giveaway ends, track and analyze the results. Evaluate the number of email signups, the level of engagement, and the overall success of the campaign. Use this data to identify areas for improvement and inform future contest and giveaway strategies.

By implementing these tips and running contests and giveaways strategically, you can effectively grow your email list and engage with your target audience. Remember to keep your contests and giveaways exciting, relevant, and valuable to continue driving list growth and nurturing long-term relationships with your subscribers.

And that wraps up Chapter 9 of "The Ultimate Guide on How to Grow Your Email List." In the next chapter, we'll explore the importance of analyzing and optimizing your email list growth strategy. Stay tuned!

Chapter 10: Analyzing and Optimizing Your Email List Growth Strategy

So, you've implemented various strategies to grow your email list. That's fantastic! But the work doesn't stop there. To keep your email list thriving, it's crucial to continually analyze and optimize your efforts. By tracking and measuring the success of your email list growth strategy, you can pinpoint areas for improvement and make informed decisions that maximize your results.

Why Analyzing and Optimizing Is Important

Analyzing and optimizing your email list growth strategy is vital for several reasons:

1. Identify What's Working: By diving into your data, you can figure out which channels, tactics, or campaigns are bringing in the most email signups. This insight allows you to focus more on what's working and allocate your resources more effectively.
2. Pinpoint Areas for Improvement: On the flip side, analyzing your data helps you spot areas that might be underperforming. Understanding what's

not working enables you to make necessary adjustments and optimize your strategy for better results.
3. Understand Your Audience Better: Analyzing your email list growth metrics provides valuable insights into your audience. By examining demographic data, engagement levels, and other behavioral patterns, you can tailor your content and offers to better meet their needs and interests.
4. Increase Email List Engagement: Knowing your subscribers and their preferences helps you craft more targeted and personalized email campaigns. This leads to higher engagement, increased open rates, and greater conversion rates.
5. Drive Business Growth: Optimizing your email list growth strategy ultimately contributes to your overall business growth. By attracting and nurturing a larger pool of engaged subscribers, you increase your chances of converting them into loyal customers.

Key Metrics to Measure

When analyzing and optimizing your email list growth strategy, keep an eye on these key metrics:

1. Email Signups: Track the number of new subscribers joining your email list over a specific period. This provides a general sense of your strategy's effectiveness.
2. Conversion Rate: Calculate the percentage of website visitors or social media followers who sign up for your email list. A higher conversion rate indicates a more successful strategy.
3. Source of Signups: Determine which channels or campaigns are driving the most email signups. This helps you prioritize your marketing efforts and invest in the most effective channels.
4. Engagement Metrics: Analyze metrics like open rates, click-through rates, and unsubscribe rates to assess the health of your email list. High engagement rates indicate a strong and active subscriber base.
5. Segmentation Performance: Evaluate the success of your segmentation efforts by tracking metrics like click-through rates and conversion rates for different segments of your email list. This helps you tailor your content and offers to specific subsets of your audience.
6. Return on Investment (ROI): Measure the financial impact of your email list growth strategy by calculating the revenue generated from email marketing campaigns. This metric helps determine the overall effectiveness of

your strategy.

Optimizing Your Email List Growth Strategy

To optimize your email list growth strategy, consider these tips:

1. A/B Testing: Test different elements of your signup forms, landing pages, and lead magnets to optimize conversion rates. Experiment with various headlines, copy, design, and calls-to-action to see what resonates best with your audience.
2. Segment Your Email List: By segmenting your email list based on demographics, behaviors, or preferences, you can send more targeted and relevant content to specific groups of subscribers. This leads to higher engagement and conversion rates.
3. Continuously Refine Your Lead Magnets: Regularly review and update your lead magnets to ensure they remain valuable and compelling to your audience. Monitor feedback and conversion rates to identify areas for improvement.
4. Implement Email List Hygiene: Regularly clean your email list by

removing inactive or unengaged subscribers. This helps improve deliverability rates and ensures you are only targeting those genuinely interested in your content.
5. Personalize Your Email Campaigns: Use personalization techniques to make your email campaigns more relevant and engaging. Address subscribers by name, tailor content based on their past interactions, and use dynamic content to provide a personalized experience.
6. Monitor Industry Trends: Stay informed about the latest trends and best practices in email marketing. This helps you stay ahead of the curve and make strategic adjustments to your email list growth strategy.

In Conclusion

Analyzing and optimizing your email list growth strategy is essential for maximizing your results. By tracking key metrics and making data-driven decisions, you can continually improve your strategy and build a strong and engaged email list. Remember to regularly review and refine your approach to ensure long-term success.

www.ingramcontent.com/pod-product-compliance
Lightning Source LLC
Chambersburg PA
CBHW050245230526
45470CB00005B/2120